# POEMS

## From A South Central La Gang Member

### VOLUME 1

By Johnny Griffin Jr.

# Table of Contents

Dedicated to: my Pain
Without such
My literature would be vague.

# Forward

My poems are not written in what is considered the traditional- typical sense of the derivative genre known as poetry. The bristles on my paint brushes are *rawer* than the usual artist. Art is produced from many sources and comes in many forms such as: pain and love. Literature that thrives from troubled thoughts, plagued by severe gang violence, paved with lessons produced from harsh mistakes, brewed from devastating times, starting from teenage years later on morphing into a difficult adulthood. Most of my teachings were administered while being cultivated in a murderous sector: the west side of South Central Los Angeles, in a scandalous treacherous arena, where it's a must that your "street instincts" are up to par.

In order to vaguely understand one's literature, one who thrives from a disastrous upbringing ... the intimacy hidden deep in the words of any storyteller, no matter the geographical upbringing, whether the conductor's life was cemented in a toxic public housing environment, versus an upscale suburban style raising, the receiver of information must be abreast somewhat of the life and times of said individual.

My upbringing was chaotic and traumatizing. Being on guard in survival mode was a constant mindstate of mine. I was raised in a primal manner which manifested into such a shoot-first-ask-questions-later ideology further in life. Adapting a self-sabotaging mindset, unbeknownst to me at the time, at a troublesome stage of my youth would morph into an abundance of drama and pain in a young life, producing a plethora of tears intertwined in incarcerated years.

It's challenging for positive thoughts of greatness and creativity to prosper in an environment and culture where conflict resolution is considered a sign of weakness; in most cases, chosen as the last option. Disarray has been my normal. In my opinion, any living being with a cultured perspective as such would adopt the same savage-like mentality I possessed once upon a time. Which I've worked hard over the years to suppress from my subconscious.

I'm not attempting to bore my audience with the stereotypical my-life-was-hard-and-difficult tale.

I began to take my unfair share of licks life had to offer, starting early as a seven-year-old child, being reared way past the realms of strict parenting. Once I reached a mature state, I experienced crippling doses of heartache and pain, the same as the next African-American male raised in the United States: unfair jail sentences and discrimination, along with being a victim to gunfire from brain-dead peers.

I thrive from a place where corruption is bolder than a colorful billboard print of a main street ad. It seems LAPD's sole agenda is to target and incarcerate minorities—black male citizens of urban communities to be specific, no matter the severity of crime, and distributing astronomical sentences to the captures in return.

I state this, regretfully. I've attended more funeral services of childhood peers and associates than the usual person has, I believe. Tragic deaths that were produced from generations of manipulation and modification of blacks' mindstates to hate and viewing one another as enemies. If that statement needs any validation? In the internet stage we live in, history is at your fingertips. Refer back to *The Making of a Slave* by William Lynch to explain the bold declaration I've made. I feel only an Iraq soldier can sympathize with the trauma and mental strain associated with participating in countless battles, combined with attending funeral services consecutively.

I've been a victim of gun violence on several occasions. Needless to say, the shots that penetrated my frame in 2004 and tearing my flesh, were not fatal. Painful, yes, but not deadly. I suffered a similar fate in 2022. Again, I'm overly thankful that time was not to my demise, as well. Every near-death encounter with the never satisfied reaper I've experienced, always left me with the same agony and anxiety I assume any human who was on the verge of taking their last breath has felt.

My troubled teenage years were spent in juvenile detention centers and institutions such as McLaren Hall—a so-called rehabilitation facility for adolescents, and Camp Afflerbaugh in La Verne, California. Those places did nothing but groom me for incarceration where my seed-of-criminality did nothing but blossom, flourishing past the realms of sprouting. Oblivious to me then at an immature, rebellious stage of my prime, awaiting to be squandered away miserably in county jails, graduating to walking prison tracks, such as Centinela State Prison where I was locked down, and confined to the middle of a cement cage. In the course of my multiple bids, graduating to yards of stone-aged guardhouses titled Folsom, amongst bitter-aged souls who had been caged in long enough where the word *hope* had been erased from their intellectual glossary. That's one of the few benefits that comes with belonging to the streets. You're a constant candidate for jail and getting killed; simple as that. Most experience both. I have a shoebox full of stories of late friends who were confined to wheelchairs before being murdered, some stuck with colostomy bags till their untimely deaths.

Here it is, an artistic piece of me, translated poetically. Hopefully, my literature will seep in intricately, transcend in an informative way that will fill my reader's soul with determination from examples of mental battles I've strived diligently to overcome, paving the way to the heart, giving insight to the controversial thoughts and mindstate of a complex individual. Most importantly, I hope the most for my reader is to gain understanding and willpower from a man who once housed a flawed perspective that could have inherited a death sentence early on in life. Or had me rotting in the special housing unit program in the Pelican Bay Prison.

Here it is. A prime declaration from an imperfect individual. And with a checkered past who had enough desire and strength through all life's trials, tribulations, faults, and failures, to manage to still produce a piece of work, hopefully that can help the next human struggling in their walk of life to find themselves and discover their true potential.

# *Intro*

This is an introduction to a troubled soul

From the mind of a tainted boy society has sculpted into a

vengeful man

It took me a while to go through what was already written

Trials and tribulations

I'm using this flawed land as my blank canvas

One of God's favorable chosen

Somehow. I'm still surviving

Where I wasn't meant to thrive

The soil where I'm planted

Too much poison for greatness to prosper

What if I died in 2004

Or on April 25th. 2022

Just another *nigga* for them to profess lies about

When I'm gone

To where blemished souls roam forever on their own

At least he attempted

To get most of his traumatic truth out

Pay attention

You might grasp just a little

Begin to vaguely understand what a complicated soul is about.

# What Poetry Is to Me

Poetry is everything to me

Words transformed to imagery

Floetry that's complicated

Something like the complicated emotion called love

Distributed so intricately

Chaos smeared with confusion

Obstacles all over the place

What is poetry to me

Pain smeared on canvas

Distributed for the world to see

Poetry to me

Me giving all of me

Putting it all on paper

Poetically for everybody to see

Poetry to me

Basically. what the ordinary can't see

The decipher of the higher power blessing thee

Detailed art so beautifully

What is poetry to me

One who can craft words that surpasses the heights of passion

The art of calligraphy displayed gracefully

Sometimes shouted with obscenities

Conveyed on my body like graffiti
This is all what poetry is to me.

# Slavery

Same savage traits as Columbus
Similar to Hitler towards Jews
Terrorize their land aggressively
Hunt for those who resemble me
Taught to view you as my enemy
Embedded tactics of Willie before 1619
Genetically modified for me to hate me
Self-destruction preferred to eliminate
Programmed to discriminate
Souls being broke started with Kunta Kinte
Reverse psychology implemented to destroy strong race
These are the tools used that will eventually result in
The death of many black men
Substitution state pen
Statistic casualties
As far as the constitution
In 2023
Chains are far from removed.

# Animals

We were raised aggressively
Lions that never walked beside sheep
We were the pack that haunted the beast
Now all the snakes and rats have come out to feast
All my distant brothers' brains
Left on stained ground. dry blood for the leeches to eat
Scavenger always peeps the scene from a close distance
If you drown
Sharks will help you out
On this cursed land
Nobody makes it out
The ones that remain chained to that barbed-wire gate
Stuck to them graffiti pavement soiled streets
I refuse to remain trapped in this concrete jungle
Tell me
How will I ever make it out?

# Fruits of my labor

I'm smokin' strawberry shortbread
In a strawberry loose-leaf
The female I'm laying with
Skin the hue of black cherry
I've been rolling mainly exotic lately
I prefer twisting in honey berries
For breakfast
I ravished cantaloupe and melon
After that
Retired to chilling
A bottle of gran-grape
Coupled with purple skunk
Ow what a wonderful feeling.

# If I Die

Some might cry
The others
Couldn't wait to tell there lies
Defaming my name as I rot
If I died
Did I live my truth or a life of lies
If I died would they cry
Or celebrate the day of my wake
When the time comes for my soul to fly away
Hope I pass the sky
Hopefully not just another *nigga* that didn't make it
That was robbed of his talent
Killed by the hands of another black man mislead
When I'm gone
My scriptures will serve as my revelation
When I'm dead
Then the only time I will be at rest.

# Peter Pan

We used to live life like a ruthless dream that would last forever
Flying through these treacherous trenches like life's a fairy tale
There was no fear never ever
The thought of growing old never
Stunted growth of the minds kept us in cells growing old
My homies that's gone
They're young in their graves. stuck in prison cells forever.
We had the thought of being gone never
Misguided boys flying wild in delusion
Like thoughts of grandeur would last forever
Just like in real life
Nothing lasts forever.

# Letter to These Streets

My attempt at making a troubled massive short

I pour my soul out in the form of ink

My blood still stain these LA streets

My DNA intertwined with my toxic society

I can't help it

Genetically

These troubled blocks are a part of me

You raised me

Brynhurst Ave. where I first clutched a snubnose 38

The same avenue I use to walk down with Tiny Swantoe

The same street where I was shot twice

I am the remains of them 762s that tore through my flesh

These streets

You've stolen so much from me

I can't explain

A twisted relationship with no reconciliation

All this in vain

All my peers' brains still stain that same dirty pavement

All this pain sole reason I can't remain

Sincerely accept my resignation

I was not meant to survive

To these tainted streets

I resign from humbly
These wicked streets
Will forever be a part of me.

# Mirror

Can you face me
Asked the man in the mirror
Do you wanna break me
Asked the kid in the mirror
Is it fear
That you see in your mirror
Do you possess
Or are you incapable of seeing
Spoke the image in the mirror
You are worthy
Recited the face in the mirror
Can you see
Encouraged the reflection in the mirror
You are great
You gotta believe
Repeated the man in the mirror
I can see
Said the man in my mirror.

# Chasing a Ghost

I Suffered this long ago
The insanity—the mental strain
All the torment and pain
That comes with
Chasing a ghost
Every time when I feel I'm near
Just when I think. I see it clear
When I swore I caught a glimpse of ...
I lose a bit of sanity. robbed of a piece of mind
Every time I decide. to chase this elusive ghost
Just when I think I'm close
I fall
Bruise my hard head some more
Costly repercussions of
Chasing a ghost
Every time I swear I'm on its heels
I'll always hear. real crisp and clear. real close to my ear
Stupid fool
You'll never catch this
Unobtainable ghost.

# Big & Pac

Is it an urban plot?
I took four slugs through my driver door
Similar to Biggie and 2Pac
What if I died that night
How long will they mourn
I visualize my life after death
Another black man shot to death. robbed of his last breath
Riddled with bullets would be the classic story
The sky would be my limit
Another nigga that died in Cali
Did they pour out a lil liquor
Hopefully not just another nigga
That lived & died in LA.

# New Regime

Silence the minorities

Make way for new regime

Social class known as homosexuality

Inflate masculinity

Embrace pansexuality

Make way for new gender categories: Tops and Bottoms

Dissipate strength. replace with feminine energy

A tender gender transcends

Easy to manipulate

Strong men on the verge of distinction

I won't fail to mention

Make way for the new regime

Indeed our new reality.

# Lost

Where do I go
When there's no other soul to run to
Do I discover truth
Or keep dwelling in false perception pity has imprisoned me in
Do I stay sleep
Or do I except the blatant truth. what no longer is part of me
Do I weep
I can't
That pathetic part. no longer part of me.

# Traumatized

We were raised on strategical lies
A crafty design put in place for most of us to rot away and die
Young black boys hypnotized
Being fitted for institutions
Blind minds
Indoctrinated envy
Embedded by Jim Crow. the true enemy
Past down to my elder peers to employ me with the same toxic
traits
The plan has been
For me to continue to distribute destructive tools to more blind
fools
The main reason why a nigga has no problem killing me
The same ideal of savage cats and vicious dogs
Modified to view each other as mortal enemies
Claustrophobic from homicides and witnessing mothers cry.

# *Out*

Will I ever make it out
Blessed with abundance of riches
Produced from natural talents
Or will I succumb to
Frustrations from urban societies mislead
Manipulated brain-dead fools
No plans. no goals to run to
I asked myself
Will I ever figure it out
Will I succeed past the realms of
Imprisoned tombs of old penitentiaries
Or will I be
Catapulted to villas in the hills
Spoils of my geniuses
Where the air is crisp and clear
Did I really make it out?
Is what I ask myself
Contemplating from ocean views
Is what I dream about.

# A Piece on "The Concern of Race"

This may just be based entirely on my sole biased honest opinion.

I truly feel African Americans barely value or truly don't understand the importance of their existence. same as Latinos. Asians. and Europeans. or any other documented ethnicity group. Truth be told. if any race is supposed to appreciate the strength in their culture. it's the negro race definitely who has the responsibility of understanding.

Young African Americans who are the quickest as far as womanhood is concerned. to abort their growing seed. cast out the father. unconcerned with the dying fact they're aiding in the alienation of their own strong race- killing of our dissipated bloodline- alienating structure and the needed discipline from the home- the unconscious behavior of typical urban women.

Female Hispanics believe differently. concerning the topic of pregnancy maintaining heritage. I've been a witness to Latino women leading protests and marches outside abortion clinics in

Los Angeles. The overpopulation of the Mexican race in LA County is evident: they yearn for nothing more than the uprising of their culture. along with hopes of a better life for their struggling families.

The most atrocious of the sad statistics are: a black man has the slightest of problems when it comes to putting a bullet in another black man's head.

It has been proven time after time. day after day. from streets to prison. from the corner to the cemetery. when dark skins connect in a hostile environment. more so than often. a funeral proceeds afterwards. A sad reality but true: a nigga has no problem in aiding in the decline of a receding bloodline. This is just my perspective.

Just a small piece ... on the concern of race.

# *Programmed*

I don't subscribe

Probably a victim of stubborn pride

My refusal to fall asleep in this modern-day matrix

Fentanyl has become the new norm of self-medicating

Pay attention

Everybody taking the blue pill

How long until

One of my so-called brothers Malcom-X me

In my generation

Our demonstration was Nipsey

Just like Hussle

The reason for my early demise will be

Too much integrity

The sole reason they wouldn't hesitate to dead me

Honor over fame

Pain for me. is leveraging my soul

The death of me will be

Succumbing to this strategic satanic plan

The internet is the new drug they use to control

Dumb niggas are the main show

Pay attention

They wanna keep you focused on things like. likes on Instagram

I forgot to mention
Time is *Tik Tok-ing* away
Snitchin' has become the new program- feds around
Not to mention
There are no rules in this wicked L.A.nd
Pay attention
They're tuning everyone in
Into their crooked program
Pay attention
Keeping us ignorant
Has always been their game plan.

Are black people my enemy?
Continuously the ones bringing mental-physical harm to me
The palms I'm expected to die at the hands of
Truth that hurts more than a death sentence handed down from
a prejudice judge
Every time. of the six times I've been shot
It was from the undiscriminating barrel of a distant cousin or an
unknown relative
Eager to see my blood spill
How they wonder why we kill
Menace II society is real reality
Another black man giving his heart and soul in the pursuit of
killing me
History repeatedly repeats itself
Where I'm from
This is reality.

# *South Central Glossary*

**All-nighter**- Grinding; selling drugs from evening, until daylight.

**Active**- An aggressive member or person who's fully involved in conflict; gang activities.

**Ball**- To attempt or successfully deceive someone in a clever manner. (You balled me.)

**Billy**- Synonym for firearm/gun. The nickname thrives from the famous "gunslinger" William H. Bonney a.k.a Billy the kid.

**Blood**- The formal saying/greeting from one Blood to another. In reference to the color red.

**Blower-** Handgun; shares the same likeness as pistol, Billy, and firearm. (Pass me the blower!)

**Bumper**- A large, nicely shaped buttock.

**Bust A Bitch**- Making a U-turn abruptly in the middle of the street.

**Buster-** The scary one out of the group.

**Character**- Someone known to behave foolishly.

**Chipped**- Somebody died. (The homie got chipped last night, smh.)

**Chili**- Money, currency.

**Citch-** In reference to bitch; used only by Crips.

**Craccin**- Mainly used by Crips as slang and articulation of what 's up; to convey the severity of a situation; a challenge, and not limited to conflict. A word used by Bloods as well (What 's brackin.)

**Crash** (**C**ommunity, **R**evolution, **A**gainst, **S**treet, **H**oodlums)- A squad of police officers who purposely targets gang members.

**Crim**- Abbreviation of criminal; substitution of groove, used by the

Hoovers Criminals.

**Cuz**- Formal saying/greeting from one Crip to another. Thriving from the related word *cousin*.

**Dead Homies**- In respect to fallen comrades. The slogan 'On the dead homies" is used to validate the severity/truthfulness of said topic or discussion.

**Dusty**- No money; broke; dirty dress attire; bad hygiene. (Girl, Micheal is always Dusty!)

**Enemigo**- The opposing side; the enemy.

**Extras**- Doing *"The most"* when uncalled for.

**Flipper/Flip**- A female who will have sex with anyone for profit or no monetary gain, anywhere, anytime.

**Flipped**- Being killed. (That boy got flipped last night.)

**Foolie or Fool**- A greeting used the same as bro/brother/homie.

**Fruit cake**- A homosexual.

**Fu Fur**- Shares the same likeness as "goofball" and "mickey."
(This dude is a Fu fur.)

**Function**- A party; *get-together*.

**Gang Banger**- An active hoodlum who participates in all acts surrounding gang activity, violence; engages in conflicts with rivals.

**Gangster**- A distinguished individual who does not hesitate to handle his/her business. Category/group in gang culture; different in comparison to Neighborhood Crips and Hoover Criminals and Bloods.

**Ghetto Bird**- Based on statistical fact, LAPD helicopter presence is continuous in urban communities as common as a bird hovering in the sky.

**Goofball**- lame; corny; an unfavorable person amongst peers; a man that acts like a child.

**Groove**- The formal greeting, slang, and saying of the Hoover Criminals.

**Going Up**- Indulging in drugs or having sex.

**Gang Member**- A person that belongs and claims a set (Gang-Neighborhood).

**Hammer**- Handgun; also coined "a Thumper."

**Hood**- Abbreviation of neighborhood, used to replace the word *good*; also used as the formal greeting of one Neighborhood Crip to another. (Everything Hood.)

**Hoodsta**- A term and slang reserved by Neighborhood Crips {NHC} {Hoodsta Crips} abbreviation of the word *neighborhood*. (What 's up, Hood!); also used as a substitution for the word *good*.

**Jerking**- A celebration/ function, at its full peak of excitement. (This party is jerkin.)

**Johnnie**- Code word for police officers; be aware or run when you see law enforcement. Legend has it, the name thrives from an infamous 77th police officer's first name, who had the reputation of chasing down gang members vigorously.

**Lick**- Robbery; a caper with the promise of producing currency.

**Link Up** - Meeting up at an agreed upon time and location.

**Loc** - Recognition of high honor for a Crip. Slang that's used in the same respect as cuz.

**Lowball**- This word varies in meaning: A scandalous individual with scavenger tendencies; in reference to someone being down on their luck. (I'm low-ballin.)

**Mack in**- To make contact; link up, in physical form or verbal.

**Mark**- Sometimes used in a joking manner, but holds the same validity as *coward*.

**Mickey**- Someone who is considered a "character" or "odd" by his/her peers. A person that exhibits unacceptable behavior.

**Off Deck-** Someone considered not reliable, not living up to expectations. (You off deck, man.)

**Out of Bounds-** Being caught in rival territory.

**Passed-** Heist, robbery or successful mission completed.

**Played Up-** The act of a woman/individual standing someone up, flaking; being unavailable.

**Politicking-** Speaking on controversial topics amongst peers.

**Ratchet-** A lascivious female who dresses provocatively. (I like ratchet-ass Tynisha; she always wears tight shorts!)

**Rat-** Used to label a female that has a long sexual history.

**Skull Drag-** To inflict crucial harm upon a human; to beat someone's ass. (I'm about to skull drag this fool!)

**Single-** Cigarette from the corner store in urban communities. (Get me two singles from the smoke shop, Newports.)

**Slippin-** Being caught by rivals on opposing sides without a weapon; lacking.

**Snitch-** A person that divulges, volunteers information of any sort to law enforcement agencies, that aids in anyone's incarceration; a rat.

**Take Down-** Meaning, you are about to accomplish a goal; embarking on a sexual endeavor.

**The Track-** Certain boulevards in LA County where prostitutes frequently work.

**Third-** Slang Crips used to represent the number 3 or 3rd, such as the Eight Tray Gangster Crips, Four Tray Gangster Crips, etc.

**Thirsty-** An overzealous individual who will do anything to achieve a desired goal whether petty or honorable.

**Toss up**- Females who are easy to have sex with. (Hey bro ... she's a toss-up.)

**Troub**- Abbreviation of *Trouble;* greeting, slang, adopted by the Trouble Gangster Crips—close affiliates of the Hoover Criminals.

**Turnt up**- At the max; full of energy; motivated; inspired. (I'm turnt up, let's hit the club!)

**Turned Down**- An individual who exhibits lack of energy; a person who is considered "not with the business!"; a man who shies away from any physical contact.

**Weirdo**- At times can be hard to discern. It can be taken as disrespect, or a sign of endearment, depending who the administer is, how the wobbler is delivered. (You're weird! You're acting like a weirdo.)

**With the Business**- Used as a question, slang, or statement to validate a person's reputation in high regards and willingness to engage in crime or physical battle. (I had a problem with these two guys yesterday. Mike jumped out of his seat to help me. He with the Business!)

**Work**- Drugs; cocaine.

**Worked**- The act of getting over on someone.

**Working**- Informant for law enforcement, whether being compensated or not.

**Yee-** Classified the same as a buster.

**Zesty**- A male that exhibits suspect behavior in relation to sexuality. One unable to differentiate as heterosexual or bi-sexual.

*nfrndspublication.com*